So you <u>really</u> want to learn

Junior Maths

Book 1

Answer Book

GALORE PARK

So you really want to learn

Junior Maths

Book 1

Answer Book

David Hillard

Series Editor: Louise Martine

www.galorepark.co.uk

Published by Galore Park Publishing Ltd,
19/21 Sayers Lane, Tenterden, Kent TN30 6BW

www.galorepark.co.uk

Text copyright © David Hillard 2008
Illustrations copyright © Galore Park 2008

The right of David Hillard to be identified as the author of this Work has been
asserted by him in accordance with sections 77 and 78 of the Copyright,
Designs and Patents Act 1988.

Typography and layout by Typetechnique, London W1
Technical drawings by Graham Edwards

Printed by CPI Antony Rowe, Chippenham

ISBN-13:   978 1 905735 22 8

First published 2008

The textbook to accompany these answers is available from www.galorepark.co.uk

Details of other Galore Park publications are available at www.galorepark.co.uk

ISEB Revision Guides, publications and examination papers may also be obtained
from Galore Park.

Preface

This book provides a complete set of answers to *So you really want to learn Junior Maths* Book 1.

Exercise 3.5 has two sets of answers: the first set are for the first printing of the pupil's book and the second set refer to subsequent reprints.

Contents

Chapter 1: Place value

Exercise 1.1: Making numbers

Check pupils' answers.

Exercise 1.2: Writing numbers

1. (a) Forty-seven
    (b) Sixty
    (c) Eighty-three
    (d) One hundred and nineteen
    (e) One hundred and ninety-one
    (f) Two hundred and seventy
    (g) Two hundred and seven
    (h) Five hundred and eighty-nine
    (i) Six hundred and twenty-eight
    (j) Nine hundred and ninety-nine

2. (a) 14   (d) 215   (g) 453   (j) 909
    (b) 36   (e) 251   (h) 648
    (c) 95   (f) 306   (i) 740

3. (a) 40   (d) 6   (g) 60   (j) 7
    (b) 400   (e) 600   (h) 10
    (c) 60   (f) 60   (i) 200

4. (a) 40   (d) 1000   (g) 100   (j) 0
    (b) 900   (e) 10   (h) 9000
    (c) 9   (f) 8000   (i) 0

Exercise 1.3: Ordering numbers

1. (a) 74   28
    (b) 96   69
    (c) 47   46
    (d) 286   143
    (e) 419   398
    (f) 316   304
    (g) 430   429
    (h) 738   735
    (i) 871   817
    (j) 410   401
    (k) 87   78   9
    (l) 101   11   10
    (m) 623   326   236
    (n) 303   300   298
    (o) 402   240   204
    (p) 524   452   425   245
    (q) 741   471   417   147
    (r) 431   413   341   314   143
    (s) 654   645   546   465   456
    (t) 975   957   795   759   597   579

2. (a) 27   36   (k) 87   101   110
    (b) 37   73   (l) 7   30   232
    (c) 218   527   (m) 59   67   72
    (d) 123   386   (n) 30   33   300
    (e) 496   512   (o) 342   463   633
    (f) 860   986   (p) 707   717   727   747
    (g) 401   410   (q) 220   224   227   229
    (h) 223   233   (r) 103   113   131   301   311
    (i) 716   761   (s) 234   243   437   473   734
    (j) 167   617   (t) 235   253   325   352   523   532

Exercise 1.4: Summary exercise

1. (a) 973
    (b) 379

2. (a) 24   25   42   45   52   54
    (b) 245   254   425   452   524   542

3. (a) Seven hundred and seventeen
    (b) 402

4. (a) 70   (b) 6   (c) 400   (d) 3000

5. (a) 66   64   46
    (b) 87   78   76   67
    (c) 753   735   573   537   375   357

6. (a) 12   15   21
    (b) 203   212   221   230
    (c) 123   132   213   231   312   321

Chapter 2: Counting

Exercise 2.1: Counting in units

1. (a) 3, 4, 5, 6, 7, 8, ...
   (b) 17, 18, 19, 20, 21, 22, ...
   (c) 40, 41, 42, 43, 44, 45, ...
   (d) 93, 94, 95, 96, 97, 98, ...

2. (a) 6, 5, 4, 3, 2, 1, 0
   (b) 19, 18, 17, 16, 15, 14, ...
   (c) 50, 49, 48, 47, 46, 45, ...
   (d) 109, 108, 107, 106, 105, 104, ...

Exercise 2.2: Counting in twos

1. (a) 2, 4, 6, 8, 10, 12, ...
   (b) 3, 5, 7, 9, 11, 13, ...
   (c) 28, 30, 32, 34, 36, 38, ...
   (d) 87, 89, 91, 93, 95, 97, ...

2. (a) 12, 10, 8, 6, 4, 2, 0
   (b) 25, 23, 21, 19, 17, 15, ...
   (c) 40, 38, 36, 34, 32, 30, ...
   (d) 103, 101, 99, 97, 95, 93, ...

Exercise 2.3: Counting in threes

1. (a) 3, 6, 9, 12, 15, 18, ...
   (b) 11, 14, 17, 20, 23, 26, ...
   (c) 48, 51, 54, 57, 60, 63, ...
   (d) 99, 102, 105, 108, 111, 114, ...

2. (a) 7, 4, 1
   (b) 18, 15, 12, 9, 6, 3, 0
   (c) 53, 50, 47, 44, 41, 38, ...
   (d) 104, 101, 98, 95, 92, 89, ...

Exercise 2.4: Counting in fours

1. (a) 4, 8, 12, 16, 20, 24, ...
   (b) 15, 19, 23, 27, 31, 35, ...
   (c) 50, 54, 58, 62, 66, 70, ...
   (d) 81, 85, 89, 93, 97, 101, ...

2. (a) 11, 7, 3
   (b) 49, 45, 41, 37, 33, 29, ...
   (c) 74, 70, 66, 62, 58, 54, ...
   (d) 112, 108, 104, 100, 96, 92, ...

Exercise 2.5: Counting in fives

1. (a) 5, 10, 15, 20, 25, 30, ...
   (b) 43, 48, 53, 58, 63, 68, ...
   (c) 51, 56, 61, 66, 71, 76, ...
   (d) 94, 99, 104, 109, 114, 119, ...

2. (a) 21, 16, 11, 6, 1
   (b) 53, 48, 43, 38, 33, 28, ...
   (c) 72, 67, 62, 57, 52, 47, ...
   (d) 104, 99, 94, 89, 84, 79, ...

Exercise 2.6: Counting in tens

1. (a) 10, 20, 30, 40, 50, 60, ...
   (b) 67, 77, 87, 97, 107, 117, ...
   (c) 154, 164, 174, 184, 194, 204, ...
   (d) 496, 506, 516, 526, 536, 546, ...

2. (a) 70, 60, 50, 40, 30, 20, 10, 0
   (b) 210, 200, 190, 180, 170, 160, ...
   (c) 353, 343, 333, 323, 313, 303, ...
   (d) 484, 474, 464, 454, 444, 434, ...

Exercise 2.7: Counting in multiples of ten

1. (a) 20, 40, 60, 80, 100, 120, ...
   (b) 55, 75, 95, 115, 135, 155, ...
   (c) 147, 167, 187, 207, 227, 247, ...
   (d) 296, 316, 336, 356, 376, 396, ...

2. (a) 30, 60, 90, 120, 150, 180, ...
   (b) 80, 110, 140, 170, 200, 230, ...
   (c) 134, 164, 194, 224, 254, 284, ...
   (d) 298, 328, 358, 388, 418, 448, ...

3. (a) 90, 50, 10
   (b) 110, 70, 30
   (c) 278, 238, 198, 158, 118, 78, ...
   (d) 404, 364, 324, 284, 244, 204, ...

4. (a) 50, 100, 150, 200, 250, 300, ...
   (b) 80, 130, 180, 230, 280, 330, ...
   (c) 215, 265, 315, 365, 415, 465, ...
   (d) 435, 485, 535, 585, 635, 685, ...

5. (a) 190, 140, 90, 40
   (b) 210, 160, 110, 60, 10
   (c) 450, 400, 350, 300, 250, 200, ...
   (d) 775, 725, 675, 625, 575, 525, ...

Exercise 2.8: Counting in multiples of one hundred

1. (a) 100, 200, 300, 400, 500, 600, ...
   (b) 70, 170, 270, 370, 470, 570, ...
   (c) 143, 243, 343, 443, 543, 643, ...
   (d) 249, 349, 449, 549, 649, 749, ...

2. (a) 1000, 900, 800, 700, 600, 500, ...
   (b) 650, 550, 450, 350, 250, 150, 50
   (c) 525, 425, 325, 225, 125, 25
   (d) 481, 381, 281, 181, 81

3. (a) 100, 300, 500, 700, 900, 1100, ...
   (b) 400, 600, 800, 1000, 1200, 1400
   (c) 5, 205, 405, 605, 805, 1005, ...
   (d) 537, 737, 937, 1137, 1337, 1537, ...

4. (a) 500, 400, 300, 200
   (b) 1000, 900, 800, 700
   (c) 301, 201, 101, 1
   (d) 743, 643, 543, 443

Exercise 2.9: Counting on in nines

1. (a) 19
   (b) 13
   (c) 17
   (d) 21
   (e) 44
   (f) 76
   (g) 100
   (h) 88
   (i) 52
   (j) 105

2.   (a) 9   18   27   36   45   54   63

      (b) 13   22   31   40   49   58   67   76   85   94   103

3.
(a) 309	(d) 677	(g) 923	(j) 298
(b) 256	(e) 799	(h) 534	
(c) 410	(f) 855	(i) 818	

Exercise 2.10: Counting back in nines

1.
(a) 3	(d) 61	(g) 36	(j) 82
(b) 10	(e) 29	(h) 78	
(c) 7	(f) 14	(i) 45	

2.
(a) 421	(d) 383	(g) 804	(j) 987
(b) 210	(e) 700	(h) 453	
(c) 466	(f) 646	(i) 175	

3.   (a) 108   99   90   81   72   63

      (b) 75   66   57   48   39   30   21   12   3

Exercise 2.11: Counting on in elevens

1.
(a) 16	(d) 42	(g) 98	(j) 104
(b) 20	(e) 60	(h) 71	
(c) 25	(f) 39	(i) 47	

2.
(a) 437	(d) 478	(g) 956	(j) 400
(b) 159	(e) 285	(h) 172	
(c) 791	(f) 113	(i) 684	

3.   (a) 11   22   33   44   55   66   77

      (b) 27   38   49   60   71   82   93   104

Exercise 2.12: Counting back in elevens

1.
(a) 3	(d) 35	(g) 86	(j) 12
(b) 8	(e) 47	(h) 61	
(c) 20	(f) 69	(i) 54	

2.
(a) 132	(d) 435	(g) 728	(j) 136
(b) 262	(e) 229	(h) 979	
(c) 311	(f) 627	(i) 560	

3. (a) 132   121   110   99   88   77
    (b) 151   140   129   118   107   96   85   74   63   52

Exercise 2.13: Summary exercise

1. (a) 18   (c) 103   (e) 601
    (b) 37   (d) 455

2. (a) 5   (c) 7   (e) 6
    (b) 6   (d) 5

3. (a) 70   (c) 30   (e) 70
    (b) 20   (d) 40

4. (a) 3   (c) 276   (e) 694
    (b) 58   (d) 290

5. (a) 3   (c) 6   (e) 6
    (b) 6   (e) 7

6. (a) 50   (c) 60   (e) 70
    (b) 50   (d) 20

7. (a) 163   (b) 425

8. (a) 4   (b) 7

9. (a) 600   (b) 400

10. (a) 740   (b) 23

11. (a) 5   (b) 3

12. (a) 200   (b) 600

End of chapter activity: Lumbers

1. 93 + 10 = 103
2. 38 + 20 = 58
3. 87 + 30 = 117
4. 40 + 24 = 64
5. 98 + 50 = 148
6. 273 + 100 = 373
7. 207 − 10 = 197
8. 175 − 20 = 155
9. 110 − 30 = 80
10. 239 − 40 = 199
11. 106 − 100 = 6
12. 555 − 500 = 55
13. 89 + 9 = 98
14. 9 + 142 = 151
15. 9 + 297 = 306
16. 83 − 9 = 74
17. 107 − 9 = 98
18. 300 − 9 = 291
19. 11 + 29 = 40
20. 140 + 11 = 151
21. 97 + 11 = 108
22. 17 − 11 = 6
23. 280 − 11 = 269
24. 307 − 11 = 296

Chapter 3: Addition

Exercise 3.1: Addition square

1.

+	1	2	3	4	5	6	7	8	9	10
1	2	3	4	5	6	7	8	9	10	11
2	3	4	5	6	7	8	9	10	11	12
3	4	5	6	7	8	9	10	11	12	13
4	5	6	7	8	9	10	11	12	13	14
5	6	7	8	9	10	11	12	13	14	15
6	7	8	9	10	11	12	13	14	15	16
7	8	9	10	11	12	13	14	15	16	17
8	9	10	11	12	13	14	15	16	17	18
9	10	11	12	13	14	15	16	17	18	19
10	11	12	13	14	15	16	17	18	19	20

Exercise 3.2: Simple addition

1.
- (a) 13
- (b) 14
- (c) 12
- (d) 14
- (e) 14
- (f) 16
- (g) 16
- (h) 14
- (i) 17
- (j) 19
- (k) 19
- (l) 16
- (m) 20
- (n) 20
- (o) 15

2.
- (a) 10
- (b) 13
- (c) 13
- (d) 14
- (e) 16
- (f) 11
- (g) 13
- (h) 11
- (i) 18
- (j) 11
- (k) 6
- (l) 12
- (m) 15
- (n) 15
- (o) 19
- (p) 20
- (q) 18
- (r) 20
- (s) 14
- (t) 17

Exercise 3.3: Formal addition

1.

	T	U
	3	0
+	1	1
	4	1

2.

	T	U
	3	6
+	3	2
	6	8

3.

	T	U
	2	1
+	2	4
	4	5

4.	76	10.	69	16.	95
5.	77	11.	38	17.	44
6.	53	12.	85	18.	86
7.	89	13.	76	19.	99
8.	88	14.	89	20.	89
9.	69	15.	67		

Exercise 3.4: Formal addition with carrying

1.

	T	U
	2	4
+	3	8
	6	2

2.

	T	U
	5	6
+	2	7
	8	3

3.

	T	U
	1	8
+	7	7
	9	5

4.	76	10.	94	16.	92
5.	43	11.	71	17.	62
6.	55	12.	91	18.	72
7.	77	13.	63	19.	97
8.	82	14.	56	20.	73
9.	91	15.	80		

Exercise 3.5: Carrying into the Hundreds column

Note that there are 2 sets of answers for question 1. The first set of answers refer to the questions set in the first printing of the pupil's book and the second set refer to the questions for all subsequent reprints. In the first printing of the book these questions did not produce answers that involved carrying into the hundreds column, therefore further reprints of the book will adjust the questions to produce more suitable answers.

First set:

1. (a) 79   (c) 44   (e) 92
    (b) 23   (d) 86

Second set:

1. (a) 101   (c) 144   (e) 102
    (b) 103   (d) 166

2.	124	10.	73	18.	133	26.	150
3.	122	11.	119	19.	125	27.	215
4.	154	12.	143	20.	169	28.	118
5.	132	13.	153	21.	210	29.	123
6.	105	14.	153	22.	181	30.	143
7.	148	15.	81	23.	129		
8.	126	16.	195	24.	186		
9.	110	17.	130	25.	207		

Exercise 3.6: Adding hundreds

1.	476	6.	942	11.	478
2.	782	7.	648	12.	204
3.	630	8.	911	13.	222
4.	545	9.	653	14.	525
5.	844	10.	655	15.	333

Exercise 3.7: Problem solving

1. 13 pieces of fruit
2. 35 passengers
3. 43 stamps
4. 86 shops
5. 235 bulbs
6. 460 miles
7. 242 people
8. 237 marks
9. 152 stamps
10. 262 sweets
11. 364 children
12. 248 items
13. 145
14. 150
15. Ali: 883, Mo: 885 So Mo's numbers add up to the larger total

Exercise 3.8: Summary exercise

1. 99
2. 55
3. 85
4. 148
5. 100
6. 540
7. 924
8. 903
9. 566
10. 915
11. 539
12. 824
13. 843
14. 630
15. 264

End of chapter activity: Doubles in the 1 to 20 addition chart

+	1	2	3	4	5	6	7	8	9	10	11	12	13	14	15	16	17	18	19	20
1	2	3	4	5	6	7	8	9	10	11	12	13	14	15	16	17	18	19	20	21
2	3	4	5	6	7	8	9	10	11	12	13	14	15	16	17	18	19	20	21	22
3	4	5	6	7	8	9	10	11	12	13	14	15	16	17	18	19	20	21	22	23
4	5	6	7	8	9	10	11	12	13	14	15	16	17	18	19	20	21	22	23	24
5	6	7	8	9	10	11	12	13	14	15	16	17	18	19	20	21	22	23	24	25
6	7	8	9	10	11	12	13	14	15	16	17	18	19	20	21	22	23	24	25	26
7	8	9	10	11	12	13	14	15	16	17	18	19	20	21	22	23	24	25	26	27
8	9	10	11	12	13	14	15	16	17	18	19	20	21	22	23	24	25	26	27	28
9	10	11	12	13	14	15	16	17	18	19	20	21	22	23	24	25	26	27	28	29
10	11	12	13	14	15	16	17	18	19	20	21	22	23	24	25	26	27	28	29	30
11	12	13	14	15	16	17	18	19	20	21	22	23	24	25	26	27	28	29	30	31
12	13	14	15	16	17	18	19	20	21	22	23	24	25	26	27	28	29	30	31	32
13	14	15	16	17	18	19	20	21	22	23	24	25	26	27	28	29	30	31	32	33
14	15	16	17	18	19	20	21	22	23	24	25	26	27	28	29	30	31	32	33	34
15	16	17	18	19	20	21	22	23	24	25	26	27	28	29	30	31	32	33	34	35
16	17	18	19	20	21	22	23	24	25	26	27	28	29	30	31	32	33	34	35	36
17	18	19	20	21	22	23	24	25	26	27	28	29	30	31	32	33	34	35	36	37
18	19	20	21	22	23	24	25	26	27	28	29	30	31	32	33	34	35	36	37	38
19	20	21	22	23	24	25	26	27	28	29	30	31	32	33	34	35	36	37	38	39
20	21	22	23	24	25	26	27	28	29	30	31	32	33	34	35	36	37	38	39	40

Chaper 4: Subtraction

Exercise 4.1: Subtraction square

1.

−	1	2	3	4	5	6	7	8	9	10
1	0	1	2	3	4	5	6	7	8	9
2		0	1	2	3	4	5	6	7	8
3			0	1	2	3	4	5	6	7
4				0	1	2	3	4	5	6
5					0	1	2	3	4	5
6						0	1	2	2	3
7							0	1	2	3
8								0	1	2
9									0	1
10										0

Exercise 4.2: Using subtraction from ten

1.	5	9.	9	17.	4	25.	9
2.	6	10.	5	18.	7	26.	8
3.	6	11.	4	19.	7	27.	9
4.	9	12.	7	20.	7	28.	8
5.	7	13.	5	21.	9	29.	4
6.	9	14.	5	22.	6	30.	8
7.	8	15.	8	23.	8		
8.	8	16.	9	24.	2		

Exercise 4.3: More practice in using subtraction from ten

1.
(a) 17	(f) 19	(k) 29	(p) 48
(b) 26	(g) 28	(l) 45	(q) 29
(c) 37	(h) 14	(m) 44	(r) 45
(d) 28	(i) 17	(n) 14	(s) 36
(e) 38	(j) 38	(o) 18	(t) 47

2.

(a) 57	(f) 99	(k) 89	(p) 88
(b) 65	(g) 52	(l) 76	(q) 53
(c) 88	(h) 65	(m)69	(r) 89
(d) 56	(i) 93	(n) 57	(s) 96
(e) 79	(j) 96	(o) 73	(t) 69

Exercise 4.4: Subtracting in your head

1. 5	5. 24	9. 27	13. 36
2. 18	6. 9	10. 22	14. 33
3. 9	7. 15	11. 16	15. 27
4. 24	8. 17	12. 18	

Exercise 4.5: Subtraction by decomposition

1.

	3	0	+	1	2	=	4	2
−	1	0	+		8	=	1	8
	2	0	+		4	=	2	4

5.

	2	0	+	1	2	=	3	2
−	1	0	+		7	=	1	7
	1	0	+		5	=	1	5

2.

	6	0	+	1	3	=	7	3
−	2	0	+		9	=	2	9
	4	0	+		4	=	4	4

6.

	5	0	+	1	2	=	6	2
−	1	0	+		5	=	1	5
	4	0	+		7	=	4	7

3.

	8	0	+	1	5	=	9	5
−	3	0	+		8	=	3	8
	5	0	+		7	=	5	7

7.

	7	0	+	1	4	=	8	4
−	3	0	+		7	=	3	7
	4	0	+		7	=	4	7

4.

	6	0	+	1	1	=	7	1
−	4	0	+		3	=	4	3
	2	0	+		8	=	2	8

8.

	8	0	+	1	0	=	9	0
−	2	0	+		4	=	2	4
	6	0	+		6	=	6	6

9.

4	0	+	1	4	=	5	4
−	2	0	+		7	=	2	7
	2	0	+		6	=	2	7

10.

3	0	+	1	1	=	4	1
−	1	0	+		8	=	1	8
	2	0	+		3	=	2	3

Exercise 4.6: Using the formal method of subtraction

1.

	9	4
−	6	3
	3	1

2.

	7	8
−	5	6
	2	2

3.

	4	9
−	1	7
	3	2

4.	31	10.	60	16.	320
5.	41	11.	103	17.	215
6.	31	12.	401	18.	122
7.	13	13.	212	19.	722
8.	3	14.	111	20.	121
9.	55	15.	111		

Exercise 4.7: More subtraction

1.	25	6.	27	11.	37	16.	16
2.	45	7.	14	12.	16	17.	48
3.	42	8.	15	13.	46	18.	19
4.	45	9.	69	14.	17	19.	29
5.	12	10.	18	15.	28	20.	29

Exercise 4.8: Inverses and opposites

1. (a) 8
   (b) 3
   (c) 5
   (d) 3
2. (a) 14
   (b) 5
   (c) 5
   (d) 9
3. (a) 15
   (b) 8
   (c) 7
   (d) 15

4. (a) 6
   (b) 11
   (c) 6
5. (a) 8
   (b) 8
   (c) 6
6. 4
7. 6
8. 8
9. 7
10. 11
11. 23

12. 23
13. 6
14. 20
15. 4
16. 12
17. 9
18. 15
19. 9
20. 21

Exercise 4.9: More practice in inverses and opposites

1. (a) 58
   (b) 26
   (c) 32
   (d) 26
2. (a) 42
   (b) 88
   (c) 46
3. (a) 17
   (b) 90
   (c) 73

4. (a) 27
   (b) 27
   (c) 62
5. 12
6. 30
7. 26
8. 93
9. 35
10. 47
11. 60

12. 23
13. 19
14. 19
15. 21

Exercise 4.10: Checking calculations

1. (a) R
   (b) R
   (c) R
   (d) W
   (e) W

   (f) R
   (g) W
   (h) W
   (i) R
   (j) W

   (k) R
   (l) W
   (m) W
   (n) R
   (o) R

   (p) R
   (q) R
   (r) R
   (s) R
   (t) W

2.

(a) W	(f) R	(k) W	(p) R
(b) R	(g) W	(l) W	(q) R
(c) W	(h) R	(m) R	(r) W
(d) R	(i) R	(n) R	(s) R
(e) R	(j) R	(o) R	(t) W

Exercise 4.11: More subtraction

1.
```
    8 5 3
  - 7 2 1
    1 3 2
```

6.
```
    ⁴5̷ ⁰1̷ ¹3
  -     2 8
    4 8 5
```

2.
```
    3 ⁶7̷ ¹4
  - 1 6 8
    2 0 6
```

7.
```
    ³4̷ ¹0 7
  - 1 2 5
    2 8 2
```

3.
```
    ⁴5̷ ⁴5̷ ¹0
  -     8 7
    4 6 3
```

8.
```
    ²3̷ ¹4 7
  - 2 7 6
        7 1
```

4.
```
    ⁷8̷ ²2̷ ¹1
  - 1 7 9
    6 4 2
```

9.
```
    ⁶7̷ ⁹0̷ ¹5
  - 5 2 8
    1 7 7
```

5.
```
    ²3̷ ¹1 7
  - 1 9 6
    1 2 1
```

10.
```
    ²3̷ ¹2̷ ¹0
  - 1 8 6
    1 3 4
```

11.

	⁴5̶	⁹¹0̶	¹0
−	2	7	4
	2	2	6

14.

	²3̶	¹³4̶	¹2
−	1	7	9
	1	6	3

12.

	⁸9̶	¹0	8
−	1	6	3
	7	4	5

15.

	⁶7̶	⁹¹0̶	¹0
−		7	8
	6	2	2

13.

	⁶7̶	¹³4̶	¹2
−	4	7	5
	2	6	7

Exercise 4.12: Problem solving

1. 5 years old
2. 3 apples
3. 5 pencils
4. 7 marks
5. 7 marks
6. 5 km
7. 6 girls
8. 9 chocolates
9. 18 chapters
10. 13 members
11. 33 books
12. 54 marks
13. 62 years old
14. 18 boys
15. 87 pages
16. 243 runs
17. 262 loaves
18. 179 members
19. 53 stamps
20. 693 miles

Exercise 4.13: Summary exercise

1. 5
2. 9
3. 8
4. 14
5. 7
6. 7
7. 54
8. 9
9. 47
10. 37
11. 33
12. 22
13. 30
14. 155
15. 80
16. 137
17. 202
18. 240
19. 252
20. 227
21. 366
22. 443
23. 146
24. 267
25. 56
26. 83
27. 57
28. 26
29. 67
30. 23

End of chapter activity: Subtraction chart

−	1	2	3	4	5	6	7	8	9	10	11	12	13	14	15	16	17	18	19	20
1	0	1	2	3	4	5	6	7	8	9	10	11	12	13	14	15	16	17	18	19
2		0	1	2	3	4	5	6	7	8	9	10	11	12	13	14	15	16	17	18
3			0	1	2	3	4	5	6	7	8	9	10	11	12	13	14	15	16	17
4				0	1	2	3	4	5	6	7	8	9	10	11	12	13	14	15	16
5					0	1	2	3	4	5	6	7	8	9	10	11	12	13	14	15
6						0	1	2	3	4	5	6	7	8	9	10	11	12	13	14
7							0	1	2	3	4	5	6	7	8	9	10	11	12	13
8								0	1	2	3	4	5	6	7	8	9	10	11	12
9									0	1	2	3	4	5	6	7	8	9	10	11
10										0	1	2	3	4	5	6	7	8	9	10
11											0	1	2	3	4	5	6	7	8	9
12												0	1	2	3	4	5	6	7	8
13													0	1	2	3	4	5	6	7
14														0	1	2	3	4	5	6
15															0	1	2	3	4	5
16																0	1	2	3	4
17																	0	1	2	3
18																		0	1	2
19																			0	1
20																				0

Chapter 5: Addition and subtraction

Exercise 5.1: Addition and subtraction

1.	4	6.	5	11.	13	16.	445
2.	7	7.	16	12.	28	17.	479
3.	8	8.	14	13.	44	18.	195
4.	12	9.	13	14.	66	19.	845
5.	11	10.	13	15.	54	20.	308

Exercise 5.2: Problem solving

1. (a) 3 apples
   (b) 5 apples
2. (a) 26 passengers
   (b) 43 passengers
3. (a) 41 children
   (b) 11 books
4. (a) 134 stamps
   (b) 39 stamps
   (c) 95 stamps

5. (a) 156 pages
   (b) 94 pages
6. 33 chocolates
7. 28
8. 195 blue lights
9. (a) 39 bananas
   (b) 61 bananas
10. 19

Exercise 5.3: Summary exercise

1.	3	11.	30	21.	119	31.	164
2.	7	12.	42	22.	106	32.	270
3.	4	13.	59	23.	115	33.	75
4.	8	14.	14	24.	109	34.	257
5.	1	15.	20	25.	127	35.	141
6.	16	16.	69	26.	137	36.	398
7.	12	17.	128	27.	12	37.	414
8.	9	18.	92	28.	35	38.	353
9.	21	19.	9	29.	62	39.	48
10.	3	20.	94	30.	195	40.	467

End of chapter activity: Board game

Practical. Use the worksheet for the game. Be prepared to settle mathematical disputes!

Did you know?

1. 800
2. 10
3. 60

4. 8400
5. 420
6. 600

Chapter 6: Multiplication

Exercise 6.1: Multiples

1.

x	2	5	10	3	4	6
1	2	5	10	3	4	6
2	4	10	20	6	8	12
3	6	15	30	9	12	18
4	8	20	40	12	16	24
5	10	25	50	15	20	30
6	12	30	60	18	24	36
7	14	35	70	21	28	42
8	16	40	80	24	32	48
9	18	45	90	27	36	54
10	20	50	100	30	40	60
	(a)	(b)	(c)	(d)	(e)	(f)

2.   (a) 3 times   (d) 2 times   (g) 11 times   (j) 15 times
      (b) 6 times   (e) 5 times   (h) 20 times
      (c) 4 times   (f) 12 times   (i) 25 times

Exercise 6.2: Test yourself

1.	14	9.	42	17.	10	25.	48
2.	20	10.	40	18.	28	26.	6
3.	36	11.	9	19.	45	27.	35
4.	24	12.	24	20.	16	28.	45
5.	54	13.	100	21.	25	29.	15
6.	32	14.	30	22.	27	30.	60
7.	18	15.	21	23.	20		
8.	40	16.	16	24.	12		

Exercise 6.3: Multiples of ten and one hundred

1.	170	6.	430	11.	600	16.	7400
2.	650	7.	680	12.	1500	17.	25 000
3.	800	8.	300	13.	3000	18.	900
4.	1480	9.	7420	14.	12 000	19.	6000
5.	5050	10.	3000	15.	20 200	20.	40 000

Exercise 6.4: Multiplication by partition

Pupils should use the partition method in their calculations. The first three are shown as example layouts.

1. $40 \times 2 = 4 \times 2 \times 10$
    $= 8 \times 10$
    $= 80$

2. $30 \times 3 = 3 \times 3 \times 10$
    $= 9 \times 10$
    $= 90$

3. $20 \times 4 = 2 \times 4 \times 10$
    $= 8 \times 10$
    $= 80$

4.	250	9.	60	14.	180	19.	280
5.	240	10.	150	15.	420	20.	180
6.	120	11.	560	16.	360		
7.	180	12.	480	17.	400		
8.	200	13.	270	18.	300		

Exercise 6.5: Practising partition and the formal method of multiplication

1.

H	T	U
	4	3
×		2
		6
+	8	0
	8	6

2.

H	T	U
	8	6
×		3
	1	8
+	2	4	0
2	5	8

3.	188	8.	348	13.	288	18.	168
4.	145	9.	156	14.	188	19.	238
5.	120	10.	378	15.	135	20.	117
6.	144	11.	188	16.	228		
7.	230	12.	216	17.	356		

Exercise 6.6: Problem solving

1. 288 nails
2. 108 peppermints
3. 288 wafers
4. 640 pages
5. 150 balloons
6. 216 eggs
7. 192 packets
8. 140 cars
9. No (there are only 144 crackers)
10. 95

Exercise 6.7: Summary exercise

1. (a) 24 (d) 40 (g) 48 (j) 12
   (b) 30 (e) 18 (h) 25
   (c) 18 (f) 36 (i) 14

2. (a) 780 (d) 260 (g) 86 (j) 180
   (b) 76 (e) 435 (h) 156 (k) 462
   (c) 147 (f) 558 (i) 328 (l) 320

3. 72 stamps
4. 96 rolls
5. 60 horseshoes
6. 144 bottles
7. 81 planks
8. 144 children
9. 135 hens
10. 250 pieces

End of chapter activity: Numbers as rectangles

1. 14 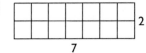 2
       7

    24 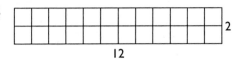 2
       12

    15 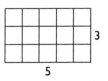 3
       5

    24 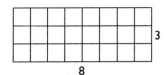 3
       8

    18 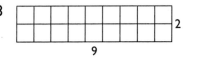 2
       9

    24 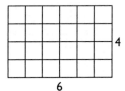 4
       6

    18 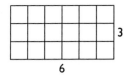 3
       6

    30 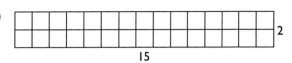 2
       15

    20 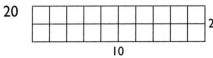 2
       10

    30 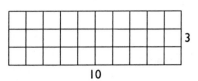 3
       10

    20 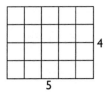 4
       5

    30 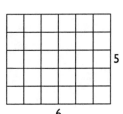 5
       6

    21 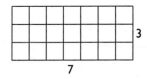 3
       7

2. 1 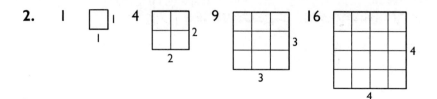 4 9 16

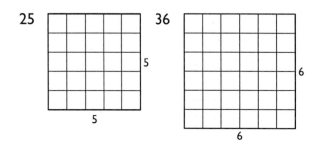

25 36

Chapter 7: Division

Exercise 7.1: Easy division

1.
   - (a) 2
   - (b) 9
   - (c) 7
   - (d) 10
   - (e) 8
   - (f) 3
   - (g) 7
   - (h) 9
   - (i) 9
   - (j) 6

2.
   - (a) 10
   - (b) 8
   - (c) 8
   - (d) 4
   - (e) 3
   - (f) 6
   - (g) 7
   - (h) 6
   - (i) 9
   - (j) 6

3.
   - (a) 10
   - (b) 7
   - (c) 6
   - (d) 7
   - (e) 4

Exercise 7.2: Division with remainders

1. 7 r.1
2. 3 r.4
3. 2 r.2
4. 7 r.1
5. 6 r.3
6. 6 r.4
7. 3 r.3
8. 7 r.3
9. 4 r.2
10. 4 r.2
11. 8 r.4
12. 6 r.2
13. 5 r.1
14. 4 r.2
15. 5 r.2
16. 3 r.4
17. 4 r.5
18. 7 r.2
19. 9 r.1
20. 6 r.5

Exercise 7.3: Fractions and division

1. 4
2. 9
3. 4
4. 9
5. 6
6. 4
7. 9
8. 5
9. 6
10. 5
11. 4
12. 8
13. 10
14. 2
15. 6
16. 3
17. 6
18. 10
19. 20
20. 12

Exercise 7.4: Division by ten and one hundred

1. 5
2. 20
3. 37
4. 300
5. 774
6. 48
7. 60
8. 149
9. 230
10. 404
11. 9
12. 14
13. 20
14. 100
15. 123
16. 18
17. 9
18. 49
19. 50
20. 600

Exercise 7.5: Informal division

1.	17	5.	14	9.	28	13.	12
2.	18	6.	47	10.	23	14.	13
3.	17	7.	16	11.	18	15.	13
4.	15	8.	13	12.	23		

Exercise 7.6: The inverse

1. (a) 7 x 4 = **28**
    (b) **28** ÷ 4 = **7**
    (c) 28 ÷ 7 = **4**

2. (a) 6 x 5 = **30**
    (b) **30** ÷ 5 = 6
    (c) 30 ÷ **6** = 5

3. (a) **7** x 6 = 42
    (b) 42 ÷ **7** = 6
    (c) **42** ÷ 6 = 7

4. (a) 2 x 6 = **12**

    (b) $\frac{1}{2}$ of **12** = 6

5. (a) 20 x $\frac{1}{2}$ = **10**

    (b) 10 x 2 = **20**

6.	**8** x 3 = 24	10.	15 ÷ 5 = **3**	13.	40 ÷ **5** = 8
7.	**6** x 5 = 30	11.	**36** ÷ 9 = 4	14.	6 x **3** = 18
8.	24 ÷ 6 = **4**	12.	**2** x 6 = 12	15.	21 ÷ 3 = **7**
9.	**27** ÷ 3 = 9				

Exercise 7.7: Checking your answers

1.	R	6.	R	11.	R	16.	R
2.	R	7.	W	12.	R	17.	W
3.	W	8.	R	13.	W	18.	R
4.	R	9.	R	14.	W	19.	R
5.	W	10.	W	15.	W	20.	W

Exercise 7.8: Formal method of division

1.

		1	4
	2	2	8

2.

		1	4
	3	4	¹2

3.

		1	4
	4	5	¹6

4.	12	10.	27	16.	28	22.	24
5.	11	11.	38	17.	42	23.	13
6.	17	12.	27	18.	14	24.	45
7.	18	13.	18	19.	31	25.	14
8.	12	14.	16	20.	17	26.	13
9.	13	15.	16	21.	19		

Exercise 7.9: Problem solving

1.	16 biscuits	6.	16 laps
2.	£17	7.	5 strips
3.	15 boxes	8.	£15
4.	9 packets	9.	23 marks
5.	16 strawberries	10.	13 overs

Exercise 7.10: Summary exercise

1.
(a) 9   (f) 8 r.2   (k) 4   (p) 6
(b) 6   (g) 7   (l) 3 r.2   (q) 4 r.4
(c) 10   (h) 7   (m)8   (r) 8
(d) 4 r.2   (i) 3   (n) 5 r.1   (s) 2 r.4
(e) 3 r.3   (j) 7   (o) 4   (t) 12

2.
(a) 15   (e) 29   (i) 13   (m) 19
(b) 9   (f) 15   (j) 14   (n) 22
(c) 70   (g) 27   (k) 13   (o) 16
(d) 12   (h) 26   (l) 37

End of chapter activity: Mixed signs

1.
(a) (i) ×   (b) (i) −   (c) (i) ÷
    (ii) +   (ii) ÷   (ii) +
    (iii) ÷   (iii) +   (iii) −
    (iv) −   (iv) ×   (iv) ×

2.
(a) 6   (c) 3
(b) 12   (d) 27

3.
(a) 3   (c) 15
(b) 10   (d) 2

Chapter 8: Sequences

Exercise 8.1: Sequences

1. (a)

   (b)

   (c)

   (d)

2. (a) (i) 9   11   (ii) add 2
   (b) (i) 18   20   (ii) add 2
   (c) (i) 14   17   (ii) add 3
   (d) (i) 13   11   (ii) subtract 2
   (e) (i) 36   31   (ii) subtract 5
   (f) (i) 7   4   (ii) subtract 3
   (g) (i) 25   30   (ii) add 5
   (h) (i) 15   18   (ii) add 3
   (i) (i) 40   48   (ii) add 8
   (j) (i) 12   6   (ii) subtract 6
   (k) (i) 18   15   (ii) subtract 3
   (l) (i) 10   5   (ii) divide by 2
   (m)(i) 45   54   (ii) add 9
   (n) (i) 21   14   (ii) subtract 7
   (o) (i) 10   0   (ii) subtract 10

3. (a) 4   6
    (b) 6   12
    (c) 9   3
    (d) 1   17
    (e) 35   30
    (f) 28   35
    (g) 75   100
    (h) 30   75
    (i) 300   250
    (j) 180   160

End of chapter activity: Test your friends

Check pupils' sequences.

Chapter 9: Money

Exercise 9.1: Using coins

1.
   (a) 2 (2p, 1p)
   (b) 2 (5p, 2p)
   (c) 3 (5p, 2p, 2p)
   (d) 2 (10p, 1p)
   (e) 2 (20p, 5p)
   (f) 5 (20p, 20p, 5p, 2p, 1p)
   (g) 4 (50p, 10p, 5p, 1p)
   (h) 4 (£1, 50p, 20p, 10p)
   (i) 3 (£2, 20p, 2p)
   (j) 9 (£2, £2, £1, 50p, 20p, 20p, 5p, 2p, 2p)

2.
5p	(5p)	10p	(10p)	20p (20p)	50p (50p)
15p	(5p, 10p)	30p	(10p, 20p)	70p (20p, 50p)	
25p	(5p, 20p)	60p	(10p, 50p)		
55p	(5p, 50p)	80p	(10p, 20p, 50p)		
35p	(5p, 10p, 20p)				
65p	(5p, 10p, 50p)				
75p	(5p, 20p, 50p)				
85p	(5p, 10p, 20p, 50p)				

3. 5
4. 55p
5. (a) 87p
   (b) 38p
6. 20p, 2p, 2p, 1p
7. 15 2p coins
8. £170
9. 1p
10. No (he is 10p short)

Exercise 9.2: Converting pounds to pence

1. 500p
2. 2500p
3. 17 500p
4. 364p
5. 999p
6. 37p
7. 70p
8. 8p
9. 10p
10. 101p
11. 75p
12. 243p
13. 190p
14. 9p
15. 442p
16. 25p
17. 900p
18. 9000p
19. 90 000p
20. 9999p

Exercise 9.3: Converting pence to pounds

1. £2.00
2. £1.50
3. £2.40
4. £1.48
5. £9.95
6. £3.70
7. £3.07
8. £0.38
9. £0.09
10. £0.90
11. £0.86
12. £3.75
13. £0.01
14. £2.05
15. £2.50
16. £0.25
17. £50.00
18. £5.00
19. £0.50
20. £0.05

Exercise 9.4: Adding money

1. (a) 92p   (d) £1.08   (g) £1.87   (j) £2.42
    (b) 72p   (e) 35p   (h) 73p
    (c) 61p   (f) 91p   (i) £1.14

2. (a) £4.69   (d) £4.20   (g) £7.53   (j) £20.10
    (b) £6.67   (e) £21.52   (h) £7.34
    (c) £6.00   (f) £3.35   (i) £14.82

3. (a) £1.89   (d) £3.44   (g) £5.38   (j) £0.67 or 67p
    (b) £2.84   (e) £1.23   (h) £3.66
    (c) £6.51   (f) £2.12   (i) £1.68

Exercise 9.5: Subtracting money

1. (a) 32p   (d) 44p   (g) £3.25   (j) £3.51
    (b) 33p   (e) £1.37   (h) 92p
    (c) 36p   (f) £4.14   (i) £3.55

2. (a)

T	U			
0	0 ·	$^{8}\cancel{9}$	$^{1}4$	
− 0	0 ·	1	7	
0	0 ·	7	7	

so 77p

(b)

T	U			
0	0 ·	$^{6}\cancel{7}$	$^{1}5$	
− 0	0 ·	4	9	
0	0 ·	2	6	

so 26p

(c)

T	U			
0	0 ·	$^{7}\cancel{8}$	$^{1}0$	
− 0	0 ·	3	8	
0	0 ·	4	2	

so 42p

(d) £1.78   (g) £2.68   (j) £32.62
(e) £13.63   (h) 97p
(f) £4.14   (i) £9.58

Exercise 9.6: Multiplying money in your head

1. 30p   6. £6.00   11. £5.94   16. £35.00
2. 80p   7. £4.05   12. £12.00   17. £13.00
3. £4.00   8. £1.11   13. £6.25   18. £7.20
4. £1.30   9. £3.92   14. £10.40   19. £104.00
5. £1.50   10. £2.88   15. £35.00   20. £44.00

Exercise 9.7: Problem solving

1. 82p
2. 23p
3. 72p
4. £2.25
5. 65p
6. £1.15
7. £16.00
8. 50p
9. (a) £2.50
    (b) £17.50

10. (a) £3.80
    (b) £6.20
    (c) £3.00
    (d) 2 (£2, £1)
11. (a) £1.11
    (b) £1.10
    (c) Sue, 1p
12. (a) £4.30
    (b) £1.95

Exercise 9.8: Summary exercise

1. (a) 235p
2. (a) £8.50
3. (a) £1.13
    (b) £7.65
    (c) £4.44
4. (a) 63p
    (b) £1.14
    (c) £3.00
5. (a) £1.60
    (b) £4.50
    (c) £3.00

(b) 78p
(b) £0.60
(d) £4.20
(e) £16.43
(f) £68.66
(d) £2.35
(e) £3.87
(f) £1.87
(d) £12.50
(e) £12.50
(f) £4.29

End of chapter activity: Shopping

Check pupils' bills.

Chapter 10: Introduction to fractions

Exercise 10.1: Recognising fractions

Answers (k) to (t) refer to additional Worksheet questions.

1. (a) Any 3 squares shaded
   (b) Any 12 squares shaded
   (c) Any 1 sector shaded
   (d) Any 2 sectors shaded
   (e) Any 2 squares shaded
   (f) Any 8 squares shaded
   (g) Any 2 rectangles shaded
   (h) Any 6 squares shaded
   (i) Any 1 sector shaded
   (j) Any 2 sectors shaded

   (k) Any 1 sector shaded
   (l) Any 1 rectangle shaded
   (m) Any 3 squares shaded
   (n) Any 4 sectors shaded
   (o) Any 1 square shaded
   (p) Any 4 sectors shaded
   (q) Any 3 sectors shaded
   (r) Any 2 sectors shaded
   (s) Any 6 sectors shaded
   (t) Any 15 squares shaded

2. (a) (a) $\frac{1}{2}$ (c) (a) $\frac{1}{8}$ (e) (a) $\frac{1}{3}$ (g) (a) $\frac{1}{10}$

   (b) $\frac{1}{2}$ (b) $\frac{7}{8}$ (b) $\frac{2}{3}$ (b) $\frac{9}{10}$

   (b) (a) $\frac{1}{4}$ (d) (a) $\frac{1}{12}$ (f) (a) $\frac{1}{6}$ (h) (a) $\frac{1}{5}$

   (b) $\frac{1}{3}$ (b) $\frac{11}{12}$ (b) $\frac{5}{6}$ (b) $\frac{4}{5}$

Exercise 10.2: Adding fractions

1. (a) (i) $\frac{3}{8}$ (ii) $\frac{5}{8}$ (f) (i) $\frac{5}{16}$ (ii) $1\frac{1}{16}$

   (b) (i) $\frac{4}{9}$ (ii) $\frac{5}{9}$ (g) (i) $\frac{2}{7}$ (ii) $\frac{5}{7}$

   (c) (i) $\frac{2}{3}$ (ii) $\frac{1}{3}$ (h) (i) $\frac{5}{12}$ (ii) $\frac{7}{12}$

   (d) (i) $\frac{3}{4}$ (ii) $\frac{1}{4}$ (i) (i) $\frac{2}{10}$ (ii) $\frac{8}{10}$

   (e) (i) $\frac{5}{6}$ (ii) $\frac{1}{6}$ (j) (i) $\frac{2}{5}$ (ii) $\frac{3}{5}$

2. Each answer is 1

3.
(a) 3	(d) 3	(g) 1	(j) 5
(b) 1	(e) 7	(h) 5	
(c) 5	(f) 4	(i) 9	

4.
(a) 1	(d) 3	(g) 8	(j) 3
(b) 1	(e) 8	(h) 3	
(c) 5	(f) 5	(i) 7	

Exercise 10.3: Equivalent fractions (1)

1. $\frac{2}{6}$ $\frac{4}{12}$ **4.** $\frac{4}{6}$ $\frac{8}{12}$

2. $\frac{2}{8}$ $\frac{3}{12}$ **5.** $\frac{6}{8}$ $\frac{9}{12}$

3. $\frac{2}{12}$ **6.** $\frac{10}{12}$

Exercise 10.4: Equivalent fractions (2)

1. (a) Any 1 rectangle shaded   (c) Any 2 rectangles shaded
   (b) Any 6 squares shaded   (d) Any 5 squared shaded

2. (a) Any 1 rectangle shaded   (c) Any 4 rectangles shaded
   (b) Any 2 squares shaded   (d) Any 3 rectangles shaded

3. (a) $\frac{3}{4}$ (b) $\frac{9}{12}$ or $\frac{3}{4}$ (c) $\frac{7}{12}$ (d) $\frac{6}{8}$ or $\frac{3}{4}$

   (e) (a), (b) and (d)

4. (a) 4 by 5 rectangle, any 10 squares shaded
   (b) 4 by 5 rectangle, any 10 squares shaded
   (c) 4 by 5 rectangle, any 16 squares shaded
   (d) 4 by 5 rectangle, any 16 squares shaded

5. Four 4 by 5 rectangles, any 10 squares shaded in each

6.
(a) 6	(d) 12	(g) 10	(j) 14
(b) 6	(e) 6	(h) 15	
(c) 12	(f) 4	(i) 4	

7. (a) 15   (d) 30   (g) 25   (j) 6
    (b) 20   (e) 24   (h) 28
    (c) 16   (f) 12   (i) 8

Exercise 10.5: Lowest terms

1. 2   6. 3   11. 1   16. 5
2. 6   7. 8   12. 1   17. 3
3. 5   8. 3   13. 5   18. 7
4. 2   9. 3   14. 3   19. 3
5. 4   10. 5   15. 5   20. 1

Exercise 10.6: Fractions of a number (1)

1. 4   4. 2   7. 5   10. 5
2. 2   5. 3   8. 5   11. 7
3. 3   6. 2   9. 6   12. 5

Exercise 10.7: Fractions of a number (2)

1. 10   4. 12   7. 10   10. 30
2. 6   5. 18   8. 20
3. 15   6. 27   9. 28

Exercise 10.8: Summary exercise

1. Any 5 squares shaded

2. (a) Any 7 squares shaded
    (b) Any 6 squares shaded
    (c) Any 3 squares shaded

3. (a) 5   (d) 7
    (b) 5   (e) 5
    (c) 3   (f) 13

4. $\dfrac{5}{12}$

5. (a) $\frac{1}{3}$ (d) $\frac{1}{5}$

     (b) $\frac{1}{2}$ (e) $\frac{1}{12}$

     (c) $\frac{1}{3}$ (f) $\frac{1}{10}$

6. (a) 12   (c) 8

     (b) 9   (d) 3

7. (a) $\frac{5}{6}$ (c) $\frac{2}{3}$ (e) $\frac{4}{9}$

     (b) $\frac{3}{4}$ (d) $\frac{2}{3}$ (f) $\frac{4}{7}$

8. (a) 15   (c) 8   (e) 21

     (b) 16   (d) 10   (f) 30

End of chapter activity: Fractional dominoes

Practical. Cut the dominoes out from the worksheet or challenge pupils to make their own.

Chapter 11: Scales, estimation and rounding

Exercise 11.1: Reading scales

	A	B	C
1.	5	3	9
2.	4	1	7
3.	20	60	85
4.	60	30	95
5.	50	25	80
6.	10	25	45
7.	25	15	30
8.	10	18	3
9.	5	12	16
10.	1	$2\frac{1}{2}$	$3\frac{1}{2}$

Exercise 11.2: Marking numbers on a scale

1.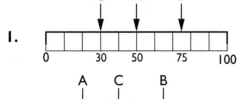

2.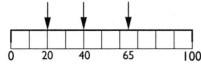

3.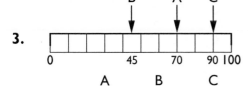

4.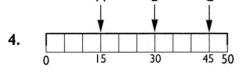

5.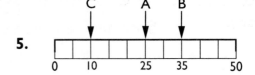

6.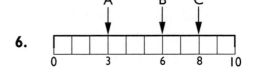

7.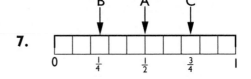

8.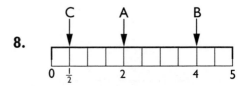

Exercise 11.3: Rounding to the nearest ten

1. (a) 30
    (b) 40
    (c) 10
    (d) 70
    (e) 90

2. 20 pupils

3. 60 staff

4. £90
5. 60 miles
6. 30 goals
7. 50 kg
8. 60 mph
9. 40 seconds
10. 74p

Exercise 11.4: Rounding to the nearest hundred

1. (a) 700
    (b) 600
    (c) 300
    (d) 200
    (e) 500

2. 200 pupils

3. 200 cars

4. £300
5. 200 miles
6. 800 points
7. 900 people
8. 100 letters
9. 500 hectares
10. 650 books

Exercise 11.5: Summary exercise

1. (a) A = 4   B = 7
    (b) C = 10   D = 45
    (c) E = 60   F = 70

2. (a)

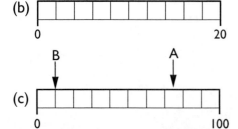

    (b)

    (c)

3. (a) 80   (c) 20   (e) 90   (g) 80
    (b) 20   (d) 90   (f) 90   (h) 50

4. (a) 200   (c) 400   (e) 400   (g) 300
    (b) 200   (d) 400   (f) 200   (h) 200

End of chapter activity: Rounding numbers

Check pupils' answers.

Chapter 12: Measurement – length

Exercise 12.1: Using measurements

1. (a) 5 m   (c) 4.5 m   (e) 1.89 m   (g) 0.65 m
    (b) 1.65 m   (d) 0.75 m   (f) 6.05 m

2. (a) 300 cm   (c) 125 cm   (e) 350 cm   (g) 775 cm
    (b) 245 cm   (d) 8 cm   (f) 180 cm

3. (a) 150 cm   (b) 1.5 m

4. 75 cm

5. 3.43 m

6. (a) 1.6 m   (b) 48 coins

7. 225 m

8. 20 days

9. 23 cm

10. 6.5 m

Exercise 12.2: Estimating and measuring length

Check pupils' answers.

End of chapter activity: Make a collection and investigate Imperial units of length

Check that the information collected is suitable for use in the measurement presentation activity at the end of Chapter 15.

You could challenge pupils to research the origin of other measurement. For example, an inch is the length of a thumb; a foot is a length of a foot.

Chapter 13: Measurement – mass

Exercise 13.1: Reading and marking scales

1. (a) 50 g   (b) A: 350 g   (c) B: 880 g

2. (a) 20 g   (b) A: 260 g   (c) B: 620 g

3. (a) $\frac{1}{2}$ g   (b) A: $7\frac{1}{2}$ g   (c) B: $13\frac{1}{4}$ g

4.

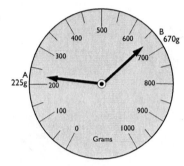

5.

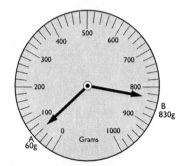

6.

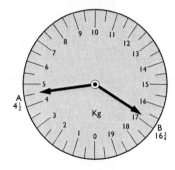

Exercise 13.2: Working with mass

1. 630 g
2. 175 g
3. 183 kg
4. 650 g
5. 210 g
6. 4 packets

7. (a) 2.25 kg
   (b) Less
8. 150 g
9. 1.25 kg
10. 84 kg

Exercise 13.3: Estimating and measuring mass

Check pupils' answers.

End of chapter activity: Make a collection and investigate Imperial units of mass

This information, together with that collected for the activities at the end of Chapters 12 and 14, will be used to make a presentation on measurements, at the end of Chapter 15.

Check that the information collected is suitable.

Chapter 14: Measurement – capacity

Exercise 14.1: Reading and marking scales

1.   (a) 100 *ml*   (b) 800 *ml*   (c) 150 *ml*
2.   (a) 200 *ml*   (b) 400 *ml*   (c) 700 *ml*
3.   (a) 50 *ml*   (b) 450 *ml*   (c) 175 *ml*

4.

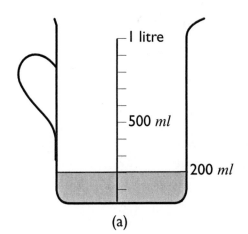

(a)

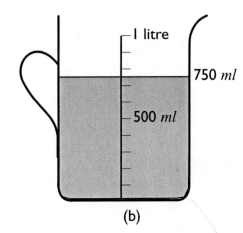

(b)

5.

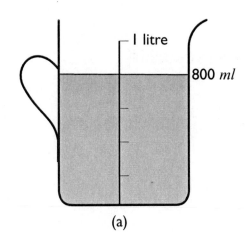

(a)

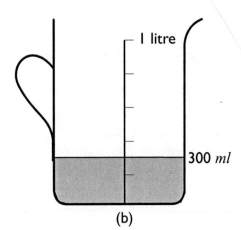

(b)

6.

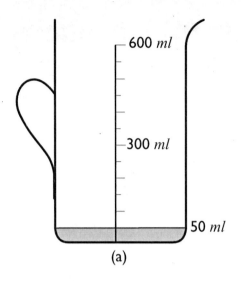

(a)

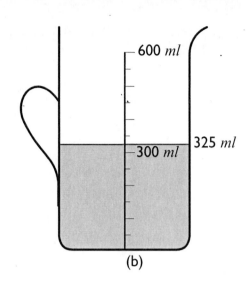

(b)

Exercise 14.2: Working with capacity

1. 430 *ml*
2. 42 *ml*
3. 72 litres
4. 425 litres
5. 16 spoonfuls
6. 725 *ml*

7. (a) 21 litres
    (b) 99 litres
8. 30 litres
9. 342 *ml*
10. 6 cans

Exercise 14.3: Estimating and measuring capacity

Check pupils' answers.

End of Chapter activity: Make a collection and investigate Imperial units of capacity

Check that the information collected is suitable for use in the measurement presentation activity at the end of Chapter 15.

Chapter 15: Measurement revisited

Exercise 15.1: Choosing units

1.	cm	6.	km	11.	kg	16.	litres
2.	g	7.	kg	12.	mm	17.	km
3.	tonne	8.	*ml*	13.	*ml*	18.	tonne
4.	*ml*	9.	m	14.	g	19.	cm
5.	mm	10.	litres	15.	cm or m	20.	g

Exercise 15.2: Estimation

1.	(c)	6.	(c)
2.	(c)	7.	(b)
3.	(b)	8.	(c)
4.	(b)	9.	(b)
5.	(a)	10.	(c)

End of chapter activity: Presentation on measurement

This gives pupils the opportunity to pull together the information they collected for the activities at the end of Chapters 12 to 14.

Chapter 16: Time

Exercise 16.1: Telling the time

Answers (j) to (u) refer to the additional Worksheet questions.

1. (a) 2 o'clock
    (b) Quarter past 1
    (c) Half past 8
    (d) Quarter to 11
    (e) Half past 12
    (f) 9 o'clock
    (g) Quarter past 4
    (h) 12 o'clock
    (i) 8 o'clock
    (j) 6 o'clock
    (k) Half past 6
    (l) Quarter to 9
    (m) Quarter to 10
    (n) Quarter to 3
    (o) Quarter past 9
    (p) Half past 5
    (q) Quarter past 8
    (r) Quarter past 11
    (s) Half past 12
    (t) Quarter past 2
    (u) Quarter to 8

2. (a) 25 minutes to 5
    (b) 10 minutes to 5
    (c) 20 minutes past 6
    (d) 5 minutes past 6
    (e) 5 minutes to 11
    (f) 25 minutes to 8
    (g) 10 minutes to 10
    (h) 20 minutes past 10
    (i) 20 minutes past 4
    (j) 5 minutes past 12
    (k) 20 minutes past 3
    (l) 25 minutes to 5
    (m) 20 minutes to 6
    (n) 20 minutes to 2
    (o) 10 minutes to 4
    (p) 5 minutes to 1
    (q) 20 minutes to 8
    (r) 10 minutes past 11
    (s) 25 minutes past 7
    (t) 5 minutes past 1
    (u) 25 minutes past 5

3. (a)

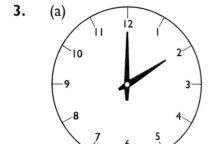

(b)

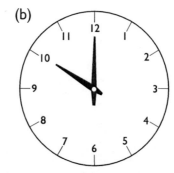

(c)

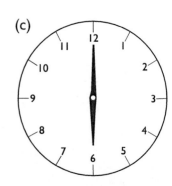

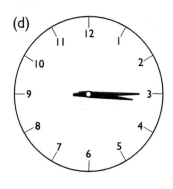

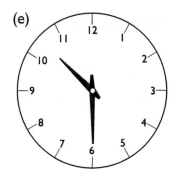

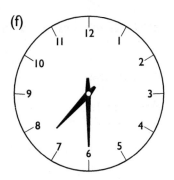

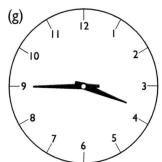

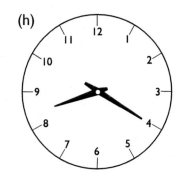

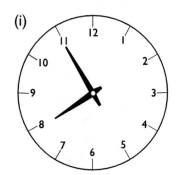

4. (a) 2 o'clock, 3 o'clock, 7 o'clock, 11 o'clock
    (b) half past 2, half past 3, half past 5, half past 11
    (c) quarter past 2, quarter past 7, quarter past 10, quarter past 12
    (d) quarter past 1, half past 1, half past 3, quarter past 7
    (e) quarter to 8, 8 o'clock, half past 9, 10 o'clock
    (f) quarter past 10, 11 o'clock, quarter past 11, quarter past 12
    (g) 25 mins to 4, 4 o'clock, 15 mins past 4, 10 mins past 9
    (h) 20 mins past 9, half past 9, 40 mins past 9

Exercise 16.2: Conversion from the 24-hour clock

1.	5.00 am	**6.**	6.05 pm	**11.**	2.20 pm	**16.**	7.05 pm
2.	3.00 pm	**7.**	11.55 pm	**12.**	9.40 am	**17.**	7.10 am
3.	10.00 pm	**8.**	1.20 am	**13.**	11.50 am	**18.**	4.30 pm
4.	3.35 am	**9.**	1.55 pm	**14.**	5.40 pm	**19.**	8.20 pm
5.	10.10 am	**10.**	12.25 pm	**15.**	9.00 pm	**20.**	12.30 am

Exercise 16.3: Conversion to the 24-hour clock format

I.	06:00	6.	22:20	II.	13:15	16.	23:00
2.	11:00	7.	08:30	12.	04:30	17.	15:40
3.	14:00	8.	20:30	13.	18:50	18.	02:00
4.	19:00	9.	00:00	14.	10:45	19.	17:00
5.	09:15	10.	12:00	15.	21:05	20.	05:00

Exercise 16.4: Writing time from words

I.   (a) 30 minutes past 9   (b) 9:30 am

(c)
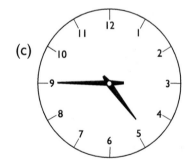

(d)

2.   (a) 45 minutes past 4   (b) 4:45 pm

(c)
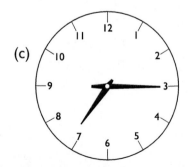

(d)

3.   (a) 15 minutes past 7   (b) 7:15 pm

(c)

(d) 19:15

4.   (a) 50 minutes past 1   (b) 1:50 pm

(c) 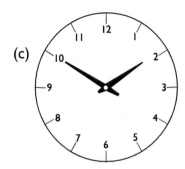   (d)

5.   (a) 20 minutes past 11   (b) 11:20 pm

(c) 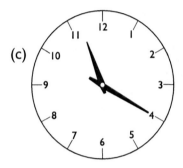   (d)

6.   (a) 40 minutes past 12   (b) 12:40 pm

(c) 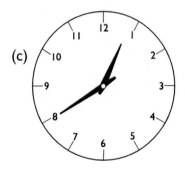   (d)

7.   (a) 45 minutes past 11   (b) 11:45 pm

(c) 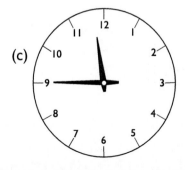   (d) 23:45

8. (a) 15 minutes past 12   (b) 12:15 pm

(c) 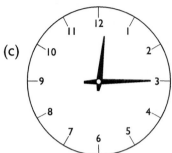   (d)

9. (a) 55 minutes past 9   (b) 9:55 pm

(c) 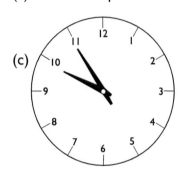   (d)

10. (a) 35 minutes past 6   (b) 6:35 am

(c) 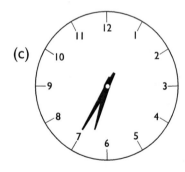   (d)

11. (a) 45 minutes past 10   (b) 10:45 am

(c) 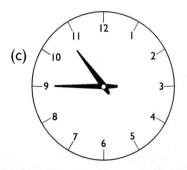   (d)

12.   (a) 5 minutes past 5   (b) 5:05 am

(c) 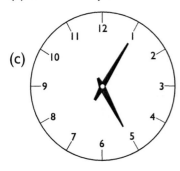   (d)

13.   (a) 40 minutes past 2   (b) 2:40 pm

(c) 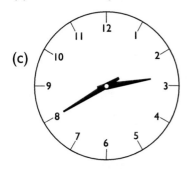   (d)

14.   (a) 0 minutes past 4   (b) 4:00 am

(c) 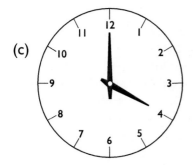   (d)

15.   (a) 30 minutes past 3   (b) 3:30 pm

(c) 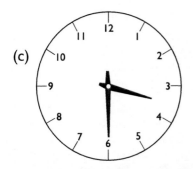   (d)

16. (a) 55 minutes past 11   (b) 11:55 am

(c) 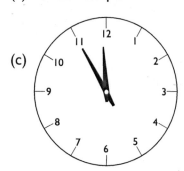   (d)

17. (a) 50 minutes past 5   (b) 5:50 pm

(c) 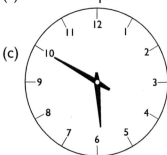   (d)

18. (a) 0 minutes past 4   (b) 4:00 pm

(c) 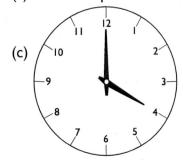   (d)

19. (a) 45 minutes past 7   (b) 7:45 am

(c) 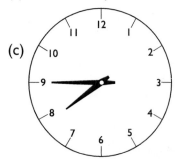   (d)

20. (a) 30 minutes past 1  (b) 1:30 pm

(c) 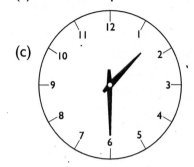 (d)

Exercise 16.5: Conversion of hours to minutes

1.	70 minutes	11.	95 minutes
2.	140 minutes	12.	160 minutes
3.	220 minutes	13.	150 minutes
4.	90 minutes	14.	75 minutes
5.	170 minutes	15.	285 minutes
6.	135 minutes	16.	180 minutes
7.	210 minutes	17.	115 minutes
8.	105 minutes	18.	330 minutes
9.	300 minutes	19.	420 minutes
10.	600 minutes	20.	165 minutes

Exercise 16.6: Conversion of minutes to hours and minutes

1.	1 hour 5 minutes	11.	1 hour 40 minutes
2.	2 hours	12.	2 hours 15 minutes
3.	1 hour 15 minutes	13.	1 hour 25 minutes
4.	3 hours	14.	4 hours 10 minutes
5.	2 hours 10 minutes	15.	2 hours 30 minutes
6.	1 hour 30 minutes	16.	1 hour 20 minutes
7.	2 hours 40 minutes	17.	2 hours 45 minutes
8.	4 hours	18.	3 hours 20 minutes
9.	2 hours 55 minutes	19.	2 hours 55 minutes
10.	5 hours	20.	1 hour 45 minutes

Exercise 16.7: Adding time

1. 1 hour
2. 1 hour 10 minutes
3. 1 hour 25 minutes
4. 1 hour 15 minutes
5. 1 hour 55 minutes

6. 2 hours 5 minutes
7. 3 hours 20 minutes
8. 4 hours 35 minutes
9. 8 hours 10 minutes
10. 4 hours 5 minutes

Exercise 16.8: Subtracting time

1. 50 minutes
2. 1 hour 40 minutes
3. 35 minutes
4. 30 minutes
5. 1 hour 15 minutes

6. 35 minutes
7. 1 hour 40 minutes
8. 1 hour 50 minutes
9. 1 hour 35 minutes
10. 1 hour 25 minutes

Exercise 16.9: Timetables

1. (a) 1740
   (b) 1540
   (c) 1640
   (d) Sittingbourne
   (e) 1710
   (f) 1705
   (g) 1710
   (h) (i) 55 minutes
       (ii) 1 hour 5 minutes
       (iii) 2 hours

   (i) 50 minutes
   (j) 1635
   (k) 5 minutes
   (l) 10 minutes
   (m) 2120

2. (a) 40 minutes
   (b) 1 hour 15 minutes
   (c) Cookery Class and National News
   (d) School Challenge
   (e) 35 minutes

3. (a) 7 minutes
   (b) 13 minutes
   (c) Elm Street
   (d) King's Avenue (on), Grove Crescent (off)
   (e) 0908

(f) 0937

(g) 0944

(h) 32 minutes

(i) 1200

(j) Bus Depot	1440	(k) Railway Station	1800
Elm Street	1446	Town Hall	1806
King's Avenue	1453	Grove Crescent	1814
Grove Crescent	1458	King's Avenue	1819
Town Hall	1506	Elm Street	1826
Railway Station	1512	Bus Depot	1832

Exercise 16.10: Problem solving

1. 20 minutes

2. 16:00

3. 45 minutes

4. 1 hour 5 minutes

5. 1 hour 53 minutes

6. 10.20 am

7. 10:50

8. 1 hour 10 minutes

9. 3.00 pm

10. 8.35 am

11. $2\frac{1}{2}$ hours

12. 35 minutes

13. (a) 50p

   (b) 0840

14. 12 hours 20 minutes

15. $7\frac{3}{4}$ minutes

Exercise 16.11: Summary exercise

1. (a) 09:30
   (b) 20:45
   (c) 04:00
   (d) 15:25
   (e) 17:05

   (f) 21:55
   (g) 10:10
   (h) 22:10
   (i) 12:20
   (j) 00:20

2. (a) 6.50 am
   (b) 5.10 pm
   (c) 1.15 pm
   (d) 8.35 pm
   (e) 2.00 pm

   (f) 2.00 am
   (g) 11.50 pm
   (h) 6.05 pm
   (i) 11.15 am
   (j) Noon

3. (a) 06:20
    (b) 15:55
    (c) 09:50
    (d) 20:40
    (e) 17:15
    (f) 11:55
    (g) 16:00
    (h) 22:30
    (i) 14:45
    (j) 07:00

4. (a) 75 minutes
    (b) 120 minutes
    (c) 100 minutes
    (d) 150 minutes
    (e) 180 minutes
    (f) 255 minutes
    (g) 215 minutes
    (h) 360 minutes
    (i) 350 minutes
    (j) 105 minutes

5. (a) 1 hour 10 minutes
    (b) 1 hour 30 minutes
    (c) 2 hours 5 minutes
    (d) 1 hour 25 minutes
    (e) 3 hours 15 minutes
    (f) 4 hours
    (g) 2 hours 15 minutes
    (h) 3 hours 20 minutes
    (i) 6 hours 40 minutes
    (j) 2 hours 45 minutes

6. (a) 6 hours 20 minutes
    (b) 5 hours 30 minutes
    (c) 5 hours 10 minutes

7. (a) 2 hours 25 minutes
    (b) 2 hours 45 minutes
    (c) $\frac{1}{4}$ hour or 15 minutes

8. (a) 100 years
    (b) Decade
    (c) 52 weeks
    (d) 14 days
    (e) Thursday
    (f) August
    (g) January
    (h) February
    (i) 7 months

End of chapter activity: Your school timetable

Check pupils' timetables.

Chapter 17: Drawing and measuring lines accurately

Exercise 17.1: Measuring and drawing lines (1)

1.   (a) 7 cm   (d) 3 cm
     (b) 12 cm   (e) 6 cm
     (c) 10 cm

2.   Check pupils' answers.

Exercise 17.2: Measuring and drawing lines (2)

1.   (a) 9.5 cm   (d) 2.5 cm
     (b) 4.5 cm   (e) 11.5 cm
     (c) 8.5 cm

2.   Check pupils' answers.

Chapter 18: Position – co-ordinates

Exercise 18.1: Naming and finding positions on a grid

1. (a) A2   (c) H4   (e) B7   (g) F5
    (b) D1   (d) G8   (f) E6   (h) C3

2. B3   B1   D2   A5   E4   C4

3. B5   F6   E3   C2   D4   D6   E1   A2   A4

4.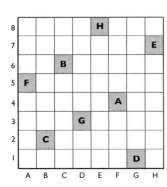

5. 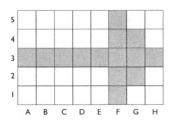   (i) An arrow

6. 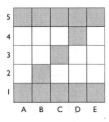   (f) The letter z

7. 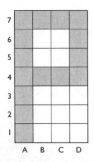   (e) The letter p

8.

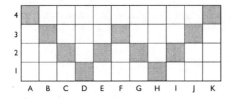

(l) The letter w

9.

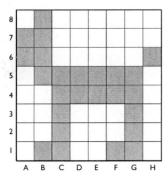

(i) A dog!

End of chapter activity: Aliens

Practical. Use the grids supplied on the worksheet.

Chapter 19: Angles and direction

Exercise 19.1: Measuring and ordering angles

1. Less
2. More
3. Less
4. More
5. 90°

6. Less
7. More
8. 90°
9. More
10. Less

11. (a) (b) (c)
12. (c) (a) (b)
13. (b) (a) (c)
14. (b) (c) (a)
15. (a) (c) (b)
16. (b) (c) (a)
17. (c) (a) (b)
18. (a) (c) (b)

Exercise 19.2: Points on a compass and using directions

1. (a) 90°   (d) 180°   (g) 180°   (j) 270°
    (b) 180°   (e) 90°   (h) 180°
    (c) 270°   (f) 270°   (i) 270°

2. (a) F11   (d) F4   (g) C5   (j) C10
    (b) E7   (e) A9   (h) B1
    (c) K7   (f) I3   (i) D2

3. (a) 5 West
    (b) 6 South
    (c) 2 East, 1 South or 1 South, 2 East
    (d) 5 East, 5 North or 5 North, 5 East
    (e) 5 West, 4 South or 4 South, 5 West

End of chapter activity: A maze

1. 4 North, 3 East, 4 North, 2 East, 1 South, 2 East, 1 North, 1 East
2. Check pupils' mazes.

Chapter 20: 2D shapes

Exercise 20.1: 2D shapes

1. (a) Square
   (b) Triangle
   (c) Hexagon

2. Check pupils' drawings.

3. Quadrilateral

4. Triangle

5. 8

6. Semicircle

7. Regular

8. A triangle

9. A rectangle

10. A square

End of chapter activity: Make a collection of 2D shapes

Check pupils' pictures.

Chapter 21: An introduction to line symmetry

Exercise 21.1: Drawing lines of symmetry

1.

2.
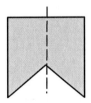

3.
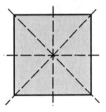

4.
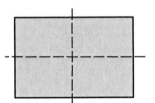

5.
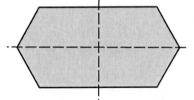

6.
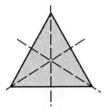

7.
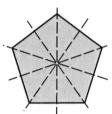

8.
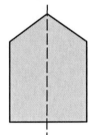

9.
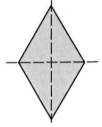

10.
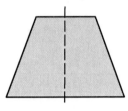

Exercise 21.2: Recognising horizontal and vertical lines of symmetry

1. B   C   D   E   H   I
2. A   H   I
3. H   I
4. F   G   J

Exercise 21.3: Completing shapes with symmetry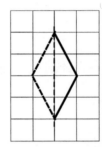

1.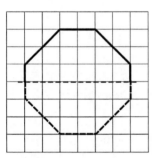

2.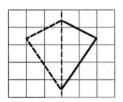

3.

4.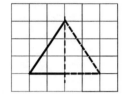

5.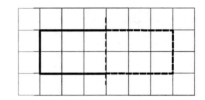

6.

7.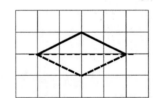

8.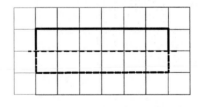

9.

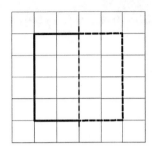

11.

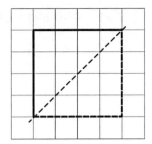

10.

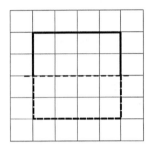

12.

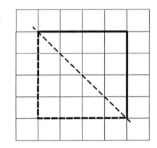

End of chapter activity: Collecting shapes with symmetry

Check pupils' collections.

Did you know?

Algeria = 1	France = 1	Switzerland = 2	Great Britain* = 2
Italy = 1	Ethiopia = 1	Guyana = 1	Denmark = 1

*On the image shown in the pupil's book the flag for Great Britain appears to have 2 lines of symmetry. However, a true representation of the flag has only a single 180° rotational symmetry.

Chapter 22: 3D shapes

Exercise 22.1: 3D shapes

1. (a) (i) square   (ii) 6   (iii) 12   (iv) 8
    (b) (i) rectangle   (ii) 6   (iii) 12   (iv) 8
    (c) (i) triangle and rectangle   (ii) 5   (iii) 9   (iv) 6
    (d) (i) square and triangle   (ii) 5   (iii) 8   (iv) 5
    (e) (i) hexagon and rectangle   (ii) 8   (iii) 18   (iv) 12
    (f) (i) triangle   (ii) 4   (iii) 6   (iv) 4

End of chapter activity: Make a collection of 3D shapes

Check pupils' collections.

Chapter 23: Carroll and Venn diagrams

Exercise 23.1: Using Carroll diagrams

1.

	Odd numbers	Even numbers
Less than 40	9 25 1	36 4 16
Numbers more than 40	81 49	64 100

2.

	Triangles	Quadrilaterals
With right angles	(a)	(d) (f) (g)
Without right angles	(c)	(b) (c)

3.   (a) 16   (b) 18   (c) 14

4.

	Boys	Girls
Gym club	6	12
Chess club	9	3

5.   (a)

	Parents	Children
Europe	8	3
America	4	12

(b) 27 altogether

Exercise 23.2: Using Venn diagrams

1.

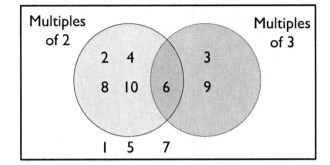

Multiples of 2 · Multiples of 3
2 4
8 10 6 9
3
1 5 7

2.

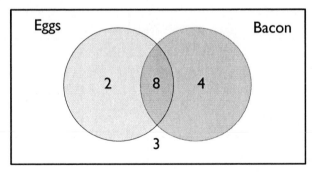

Pair of equal sides · A right angle
(a) (e) (d) (b)
(c)

3. (a) 3 children   (d) 2 children
     (b) 9 children   (e) 21 children
     (c) 10 children

4. (a)

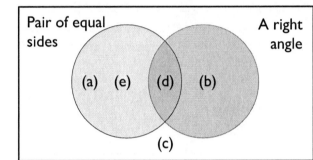

Eggs · Bacon
2 8 4
3

     (b) 17 cubs

5. (a)

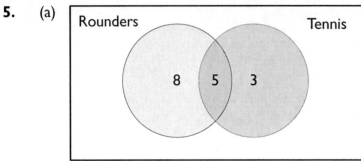

(b) 16 girls

End of chapter activity: Conducting a survey and recording the results

Check pupils' Venn diagrams.

Chapter 24: Handling data

Exercise 24.1: Understanding pictograms

1.   (a) Fiona   (c) 3 more
     (b) 0 coins   (d) 24 coins

2.   (a) 1 boy   (e) 3 girls
     (b) 8 boys   (f) 33 children
     (c) 7 girls   (g) 1 more
     (d) Reception

3.   (a) 10 tickets   (e) 10 more
     (b) 5 tickets   (f) 190 tickets
     (c) 75 tickets   (g) £95
     (d) Miss Aisle

4.

Yellow	● ● ● ●	
Green	● ●	
Blue	● ● ● ◖	
Orange	●	
Pink	● ● ●	
Purple	● ◖	
Red	● ◖	
Brown	● ● ◖	

● = 2 sweets

Pictogram to show the different coloured sweets in a packet

5.

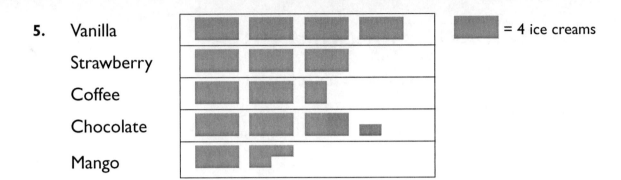

Vanilla

Strawberry

Coffee

Chocolate

Mango

= 4 ice creams

Pictogram to show the different flavours of ice cream Benito sells to a party of children

Exercise 24.2: Understanding bar charts

1. (a) 20 bottles (c) 4 left
    (b) 5 more   (d) £3.50

2. (a) 10 squares (c) Car   (e) 7 more
    (b) 1 pupil   (d) 14 pupils (f) 138 pupils

3.

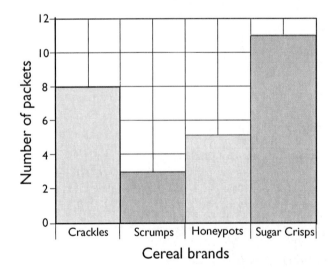

Bar chart to show the different brands of cereal sold by the village shop

4.

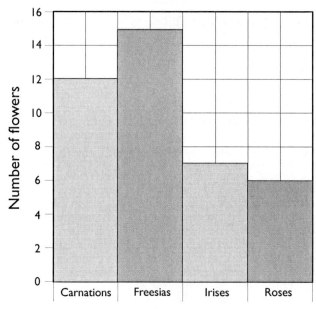

Bar chart to show the different flowers in a bouquet

5.

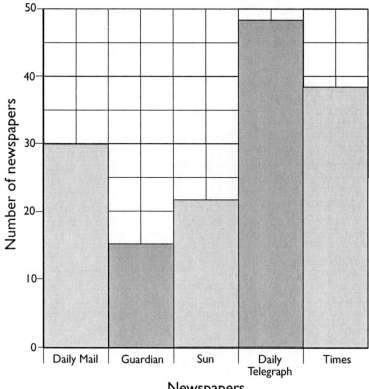

Bar chart to show the sale of newspapers

Exercise 24.3: Understanding frequency graphs

1. (a)

Number of goals	Tally	Frequency
0	I I	2
I	I I	2
2	THL	5
3	I I	2
4	I	I
	Total	12

(b) *Number of goals scored in each match*

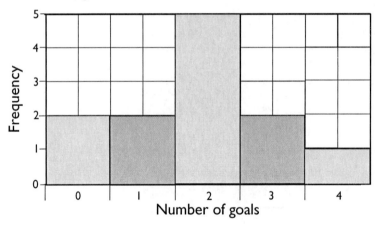

2. (a)

Drink	Tally	Frequency
Blackcurrant	THL THL	10
Lemon	THL THL II	12
Orange	THL THL III	13
Water	THL II	7
	Total	42

(b) *Flavours of drink chosen at break*

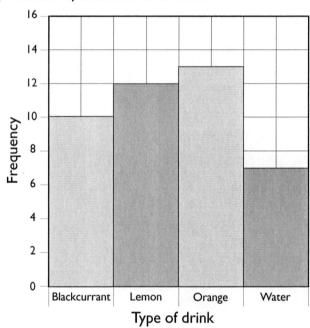

3. (a)

Number on die	Tally	Frequency
1	THL II	7
2	THL THL	10
3	THL IIII	9
4	THL II	7
5	THL III	8
6	THL IIII	9
	Total	50

(b) *Results of rolling a die 50 times*

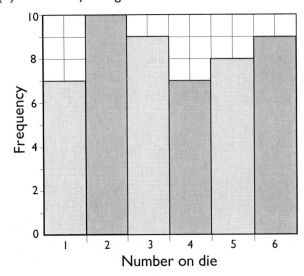

4. (a)

Mark	Tally	Frequency
45%–49%	I	I
50%–54%	III	3
55%–59%		
60%–64%	THL	5
65%–69%	THL I	6
70%–74%	III	3
75%–79%	II	2
	Total	20

(b) *Maths exam results*

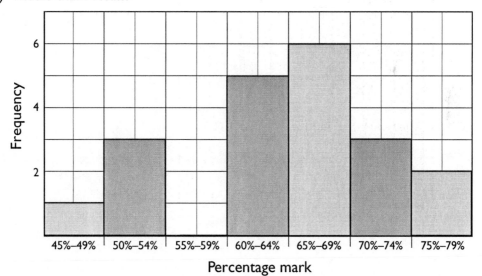

5. (a)

Height (cm)	Tally	Frequency
130–134	I	1
135–139	II	2
140–144	III	3
145–149	IIII	4
150–154	~~IIII~~ I	6
155–159	III	3
160–164	I	1
	Total	20

(b) *Pupil's height*

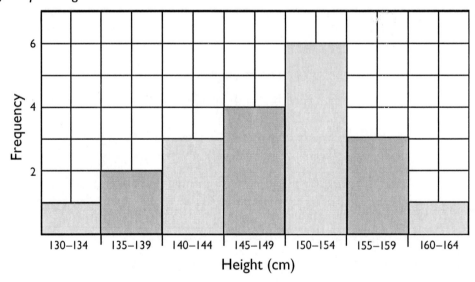

End of chapter activity: More graphs!

Check pupils' work.

Chapter 25: Mental strategies

Exercise 25.1: Using addition strategies

1.	98	9.	176	17.	209	25.	580
2.	79	10.	169	18.	923	26.	598
3.	81	11.	142	19.	684	27.	602
4.	58	12.	112	20.	967	28.	752
5.	123	13.	170	21.	452	29.	600
6.	148	14.	156	22.	728	30.	902
7.	132	15.	92	23.	817		
8.	164	16.	312	24.	379		

Exercise 25.2: Doubling

1.	110	6.	161	11.	360	16.	550
2.	170	7.	176	12.	420	17.	920
3.	140	8.	134	13.	385	18.	730
4.	142	9.	53	14.	430	19.	756
5.	123	10.	145	15.	780	20.	1000

Exercise 25.3: Addition using a number line

1.	181	9.	156	17.	870	25.	170
2.	105	10.	163	18.	914	26.	600
3.	121	11.	246	19.	964	27.	272
4.	175	12.	574	20.	982	28.	898
5.	85	13.	342	21.	161	29.	950
6.	83	14.	430	22.	209	30.	825
7.	152	15.	729	23.	165		
8.	111	16.	900	24.	184		

Exercise 25.4: Subtracting by 'counting on'

1.	4	6.	5	11.	5	16.	7
2.	5	7.	5	12.	6	17.	9
3.	7	8.	5	13.	5	18.	9
4.	6	9.	7	14.	4	19.	8
5.	7	10.	11	15.	8	20.	7

Exercise 25.5: Subtraction with a number line (1)

1.	21	6.	46	11.	79	16.	232
2.	28	7.	44	12.	86	17.	185
3.	44	8.	78	13.	108	18.	252
4.	47	9.	117	14.	218	19.	183
5.	36	10.	151	15.	164	20.	511

Exercise 25.6: Subtracting by 'counting back'

1.	6	6.	8	11.	6	16.	12
2.	7	7.	8	12.	9	17.	14
3.	7	8.	11	13.	9	18.	9
4.	9	9.	7	14.	7	19.	8
5.	4	10.	9	15.	6	20.	8

Exercise 25.7: Subtraction with a number line (2)

1.	24	6.	32	11.	64	16.	26
2.	25	7.	25	12.	88	17.	73
3.	15	8.	21	13.	286	18.	445
4.	36	9.	24	14.	276	19.	397
5.	27	10.	33	15.	387	20.	504

Exercise 25.8: Multiplication by partition

1.	96	6.	280	11.	288	16.	1024
2.	102	7.	161	12.	966	17.	1462
3.	108	8.	153	13.	875	18.	1311
4.	315	9.	230	14.	928	19.	1178
5.	108	10.	348	15.	972	20.	2756

Exercise 25.9: Multiplying using factors

1.	216	6.	416	11.	2205	16.	966
2.	360	7.	912	12.	1325	17.	2220
3.	1050	8.	2240	13.	1494	18.	3456
4.	1080	9.	555	14.	1608	19.	1944
5.	308	10.	2016	15.	1520	20.	1512

Exercise 25.10: Multiplying using doubling

1. 156
2. 138
3. (a) (ii) 90
    (iii) 180
    (iv) 360
    (v) 720
    (b) (i) 540
    (ii) 855

4. 1080
5. 1440
6. 1395
7. 1575

Exercise 25.11: Division

1. 7
2. 45
3. 6
4. 70
5. 12
6. 22
7. 48
8. 45

9. 39
10. 25
11. 19
12. 33
13. 25
14. 16
15. 52
16. 47

17. 30
18. 50
19. 46
20. 16
21. 19
22. 14
23. 15
24. 14

25. 17
26. 54
27. 32
28. 37
29. 57
30. 43

Notes

Notes

Notes

Notes

Notes